# Architecture,

## AND

## HOW IT AROSE;

## With a Model for the Gothic.

BY CHARLOTTE A. POUND.

———✠———

LONDON:
E. MARLBOROUGH & Co., 51, OLD BAILEY.
R. MEDLEY, VENTNOR, I.W.
1880.

In the interest of creating a more extensive selection of rare historical book reprints, we have chosen to reproduce this title even though it may possibly have occasional imperfections such as missing and blurred pages, missing text, poor pictures, markings, dark backgrounds and other reproduction issues beyond our control. Because this work is culturally important, we have made it available as a part of our commitment to protecting, preserving and promoting the world's literature. Thank you for your understanding.

# Architecture: and How it Arose.

## PREFACE.

The remarks contained in the following pages, upon Architecture generally, and Gothic Architecture in particular, have occured to the writer, from an early admiration of the subject, and from the study of the laws of symmetry and proportion; which laws, govern everything created in nature or imitated in art.

To define proportion is merely to state, that it is the length, breadth, and height, of objects, so assimilated, or placed in contrast, that the contour of that particular measurement is alone pleasing to the eye.

We find a due proportion of the length and height equally displayed in the stately stag, the noble mansion, and the well-built ship. There is also a proportion of the useful kind, and we can admire the humble shed which shelters the poor man's cow; but in a building erected for the worship of God, as a house of prayer, we turn to the highest form of all due proportion.

# ARCHITECTURE,
# AND HOW IT AROSE.

THE great Architect, Infinite, Divine, dwells in and about, not under, the shelter of His own Arch, which we call Heaven. "Heaven is my Throne." Heaven is everywhere, above, beneath, around, to us an illimitable space. So is God, He fills all space.

The same great God made man after His own image, to dwell upon a world of His own creation, decorated and adorned by perfect symmetry and beauty. But man had not divine power, and his earthly nature had to be provided for; for this purpose the faculty of constructiveness and materials for the use of that faculty were given, to enable man to build his own place of abode, and to adapt it to climate and circumstance.

The Kraal of the Hottentot indicates the idea of man's first effort to shelter himself from heat and cold; the hut of the Esquimaux also is simply an Arch of snow, in imitation of the Arch above. But man became social, he required shelter for his family, and friends; his ideas expanded, until in each civilized country dwellings multiplied, Palaces for the rich, Cottages for the poor.

But the proportions of a building, wherein men could meet and adore their Maker, were not thought of, and His House needed something beyond man's unaided efforts. When in Israel wars and bloodshed for a time had ceased and "the land had rest," God commanded Solomon to "build a Temple to His honour and glory." For this building every minute detail was given by God, and it is *"observable" that in the proportions of length, breadth, and height, "the number three recurs continually." Shewing it to be "typical of the Church built by the Divine Solomon, Jesus Christ, to the glory of the Triune God." The standard of measurement was the same as had been previously given for both the Ark, and the Tabernacle in the wildnerness, viz., a cubit, or the length of the arm from the tip of the finger to the elbow.

* Wordsworth's Commentary, Vol. 3. 1 Kings, vi. 2.

This Temple built in Jerusalem, B.C. 1000 years, surpassed in splendour all that had ever before existed; and no wonder, when at Heaven's command earth's richest treasures were poured forth—although even this in time was doomed to perish! Egypt, Babylon, and Nineveh, had in former ages their proud monuments, but architecture more sublime was to enrich the world with buildings of interest before unknown. Greece and Rome appear in succession to have imitated what remained of Solomon's work; hence, we find in Athens and in Rome, the stately Pillar, Frieze, and Capital: but these structures were for the worship of false gods, and a sublimer form, with its heavenward pointed arch, was destined to exalt and raise upward our ideas. Master masons, with master minds combined. Industry, genius, and almost inspiration guided the chisel and the hammer of the architect; Kings, princes, and people, gave their offerings, and it is remarkable that this great movement commenced the same period after the coming of Christ as the building of Solomon's Temple had preceded it, A.D. 1000, so that within twelve hundred years after the time of our Saviour, the various Countries of Europe were richly studded with those splendid churches, which are both our wonder and admiration.

For these Christian Churches let us endeavour to find a model, since specific measurements were not vouchsafed from Heaven.

It is said that the laws of Gothic Architecture are "lost," the principles of its symmetry and proportions are "unknown," inasmuch as the Society of Masons retain only the name of "Freemasons" with their "Lodges"; *"no drawings or plans can in any muniment room be found," although "numerous records are preserved," and the names and residences of some of the builders known, as York for instance, whence emanated plans, instructions, and workmen.

In the absence of their correct standard of measurement we will attempt to supply the deficiency.

A recent writer† upon Church Architecture has advanced the idea that the ground plan may be ascribed to two Geometrical Figures, the Oval, and Triangle, both of which bore a mystical meaning. This proportion is correct, but whence the windows, doors, and various parts of the whole? Some conjecture that Gothic Architecture arose from the form of a ship, others that a forest of graceful trees

* Britton's Dictionary of Architecture. † The Rev. Mackenzie E. C. Walcott, B.D., F.S.A.

would suggest Pillars and Arches; but there is nothing definite in measurement. It remains then for us to look further for a model, and (remembering it has been said "the *"proper study for mankind is man") contemplate the last finished work of His hands who made all things.

We are told in history, that the ancient Greeks made the human body the great object of their admiration, almost of their adoration; hence the noble proofs of the Sculptor's genius, surviving the decay of time, which made the marble all but breathe. In the time of Isaiah, cherished Images were made †"according to the beauty of a man:"‡ let us see if this can be applied to a building to shelter man, as well as to a base idol for heathen worship.

It is clear that the early Churches in our land, were constructed after what is known of man's primitive abode, with the rounded Arch, so familiar in "Norman Architecture." From the Continent, probably Italy, whence came our early Christian teachers, came also the exalted Gothic. Let us use the idea he "maketh it according to the beauty of a man" in a higher sense and trace the style called "Cruciform," not only to the Cross, but to Him who took upon Him our

* Pope's Essay on man.    † Isaiah xliv. 13.    ‡ As they are now in heathen countries.

earthly form, and hung upon it; whether designedly or not, on this plan most of our Churches and Cathedrals are built, so that not only the ground plan, but the whole structure may be tested by the human figure as to its principles of symmetry and proportion; the Hand which forms the Arch, is itself the perfect model for that Arch. To illustrate the subject we will first consider one of our most simple Village Churches; the usual form is without Transepts thus—the shape of a man—

With Transepts thus—the rounded Chancel or Apse being the oldest form of building*

---

\* The Chancel is frequently found inclined at a slight angle with the Nave, which surely speaks of the drooping head, although otherwise accounted for.

And with length of Nave and breadth of Transepts equal, thus—

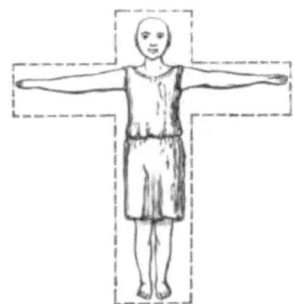

There are few instances of the latter dimensions.

Next imagine the human figure recumbent, with arms upraised thus—

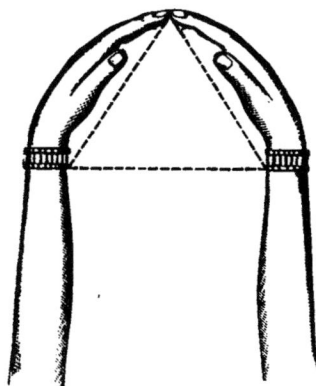

an Arch is formed which gives the altitude of the Chancel Arch and Roof, and distinctly defines the form.

12

The hands thus, are suggestive of Arches of every size, and will be the proportion for the Windows. The width of the wrist will determine the space between the Windows, for Buttresses, while the elbow and hand would propose themselves as props.

The knee upraised to the height of the elbow, gives both altitude and form for the Entrance Porch, and the feet shew the relative size for the Western Entrance, or Great Door. The figure added erect supplies the height of the Tower as thus exemplified, and the hand compressed the Pinnacle or distant Spire.

 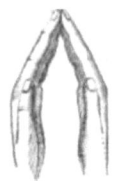

This idea of proportion, may be further worked out, so that the eye once directed to it will find in our frames resemblances to various Gothic Mouldings, such as are found in our most finished Churches. This can be easily tested by comparing the curvatures and angles made by the figure and Hand with their beautiful Windows and Arches. It would be a happy conception if so simple a model could guide the builder and the architect, since in the absence of such rules of harmony, it is only possible to copy other Churches, or work out a difficult problem.

We have assumed before that the Triangle is correct, ("The Mystical Triangle," as being a symbol of the Trinity of the Godhead.) Although architects do not fully admit this theory, its application to the human figure may assist in its further recognition.

It has appeared in the devices already given (p.p. 10, 11) is now shewn in the hand as suggestive of tracery for Windows, thus—and will again be alluded to.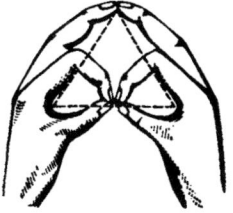

The ideas advanced are further pourtrayed in the accompanying sketch of the Ground Plan of one of our most perfect Gothic Churches, Salisbury Cathedral. The head occupies the East end or Chancel, corresponding to the Holy of Holies in the Jewish Tabernacle. The arms occupy the Transepts as waiting servants. The body the Nave— or "Body," as so called in ecclesiastical documents.

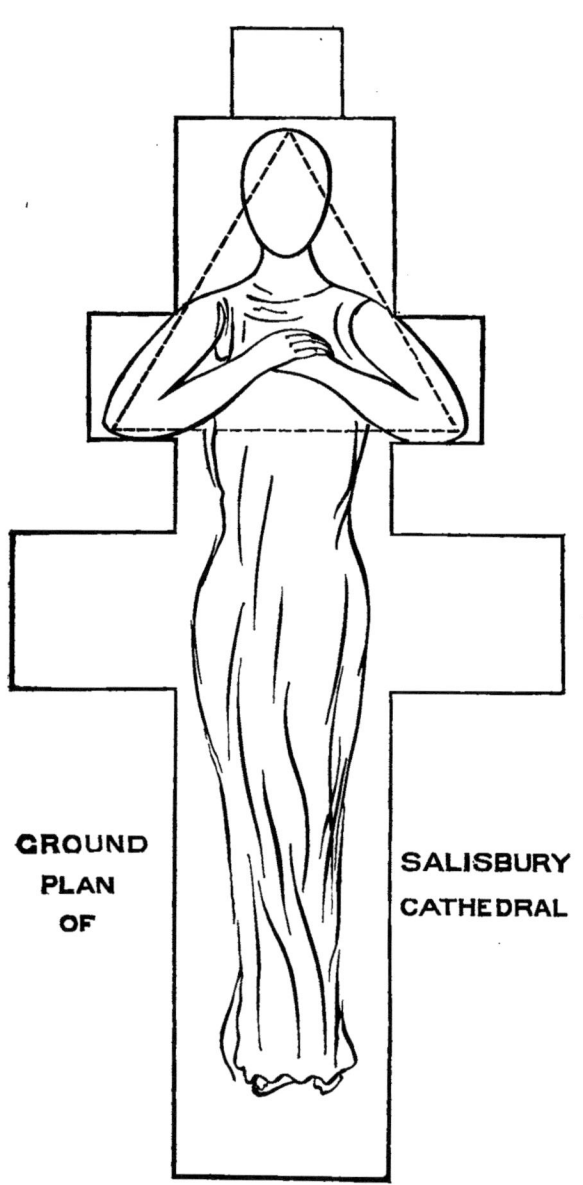

GROUND PLAN OF SALISBURY CATHEDRAL

The space at the east end of the figure has probably been given to balance the great height of the spire, while over the western space, the two Towers are built.

One equilateral triangle is shewn in the sketch, a second would be formed from the outstretched arms as the base, to the feet as the apex. The first triangle gives the height of the Chancel Arch and Roof; the second that of the Tower, for which the two extra Transepts are built to give foundation; and also they afford an area for monuments, &c. While it is difficult to conceive so great a work, it is still clear that by multiplying each part of the model, the lofty task might be accomplished, and that ingenious combinations might produce such great results. In the immense height of the structure the rood loft, clerestory, &c., would naturally find their place, giving light and lightness above; also for the performance of the daily services needful additions were required, as Presbytery, Lavatory, Chapter House, &c., all tending to enrich the building in ecclesiastical forms.

We have spoken of tracery, to which Geometry with its graceful lines lends its aid, but which the human hand suggests.

16

We now add, that although Trees combining strength, support, and elegance, greatly resemble the groined roof and cloistered walk, yet even for this support our model is not wanting, thus.—

Other forms could be produced, but sufficient has been said for the intended purpose, the writer being only desirous to open the subject, leaving it to greater minds, should they not despise it, to develop further details.

In studying the various Churches, even of our own land, all must acknowledge, that, with whatever helps the builders were endowed, great and wonderful were the minds which guided feeble hands in adding Stone to Stone, and Arch to Arch, until Pillared Nave and Vaulted Roof seem more in unison with Heavenly, than earthly Courts.

The mighty piles, calm and majestic, remind one of profound sleepers, undisturbed by the busy throng of worshippers, or admirers, who tread their sacred floors. May England ever guard these precious monuments of by-gone days, and most sacred shrines of her religious faith, until the summons shall be given for her stately tombs to give up their honoured dead.

There is a reverse in every picture, and even in the study of our Model Churches are to be seen representations of faces defaced by Satan's image: these found their positions as outer Corbels, or were placed only in contrast within to what is most divine. Man's outward form is symmetrical, and he was made for Heaven, but is sometimes so debased by an immoral sinful nature that the study of his imperfections amongst the builders themselves, or the outer world, might cause them to destroy their designs.

Having spoken of the laws of proportion as to length, breadth, and height, we will conclude by reminding our readers that these are to be equal "in the walls of the Heavenly City (made for the abode of spiritual beings) the New Jerusalem measured by a cubit, according to the measure of a man, that is an Angel."\*

\* Rev. xxi. 16, 17.

Printed by Libri Plureos GmbH in Hamburg, Germany